SECOND EDITION

Storybook 8

The
Numbers and Colors Book

by Sue Dickson

Illustrations by Norma Portadino, Jean Hamilton, Chip Neville and Kerstin Upmeyer

Printed in the United States of America

Modern Curriculum Press, an imprint of Pearson Learning
299 Jefferson Road, P.O. Box 480, Parsippany, NJ 07054
1-800-321-3106 / www.pearsonlearning.com

ISBN: 1-56704-518-9 (Volume 8)

M N—CJK—10

Table of Contents
Raceway Step 21

2

Red ?
Green ? Blue ?
Five ? Four ? Two ?
The Winner is Who ?

Vocabulary

1. red	12. two	23. third
2. orange	13. three	24. fourth
3. yellow	14. four	25. fifth
4. green	15. five	26. sixth
5. blue	16. six	27. seventh
6. purple	17. seven	28. eighth
7. brown	18. eight	29. ninth
8. black	19. nine	30. tenth
9. white	20. ten	Story Word
10. pink	21. first	31. video
11. one	22. second	

"See the video game," said Tom. "It is a boat race with one, two, three, four, five, six, seven, eight, nine, ten boats !"

"Go, boats, go!" cried Jim. "The red boat is first. The yellow boat is second. Look! The blue boat is third, and the orange boat is fourth. The green boat is fifth."

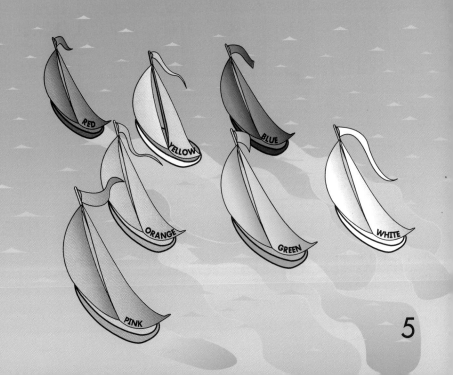

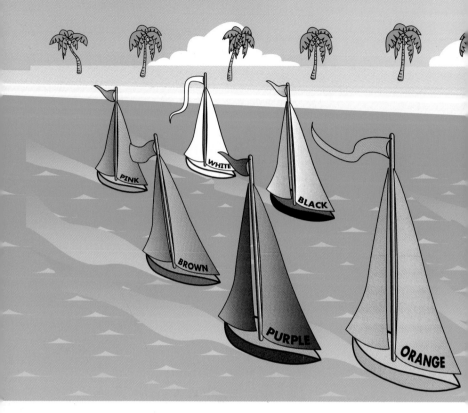

Tom said to Jim, "Look at that purple boat! The purple boat is sixth. The brown boat is seventh. The black boat is eighth. The white boat is ninth, and the pink boat is tenth!"

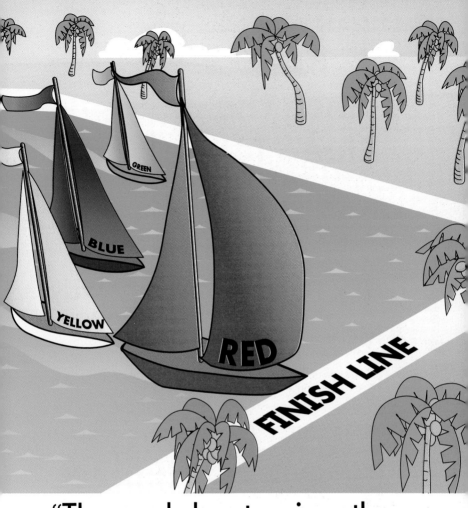

"The red boat wins the race!" cried Jim. "One, two, three, four, five, six, seven, eight, nine, ten boats! What fun!"

The End

Ray and the Blue Jay

in rhyme

ay

Vocabulary

1. day
2. May
3. Ray
4. way

a   way
5. away
6. bay
7. hay
8. jay
9. stay

any way
10. anyway
11. lay
12. pay
13. clay
14. Kay
15. say
16. play

Story Word
17. chase
18. this

8

On a nice hot day
in May,

Ray went to swim
in the bay.

He was very glad
that day,

When he went by a
stack of hay.

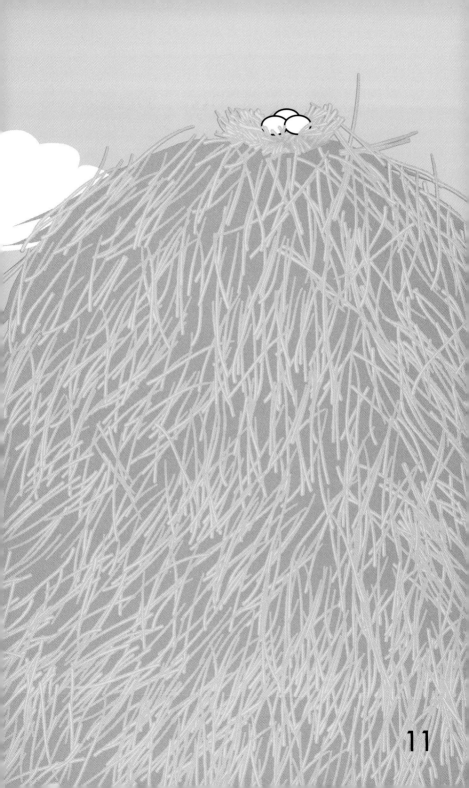

11

On the hay was
a big blue jay.

She came fast at
little Ray !

"I will peck you,
little Ray,

If you do not
stay away!"

13

"Stay away !
Please stay away !
In this nest
my eggs I lay !"

15

"I will stay away,
dear jay,

I will use some
of my pay,

And I will buy
a box of clay."

17

"I will make a clay blue jay.

I will name my blue jay, Kay."

18

"Kay will not say,
'jay-jay, jay-jay.'
She will not chase
the kids away."

"She will sit and she will stay.

She will not lay eggs on the hay."

"She will not speak
and will not play,

But I will like her
anyway."

Good-bye little Ray !

"Tell me, tell me,
what do you say ?

Will you like my
clay blue jay ?"

"Good-bye, blue jay; have a nice day !"

The End

The Shy Giant

$$y = \bar{i}$$
$$g = j$$

Vocabulary

1. cry

   cry ing
2. crying

3. fly

4. why

5. fry

6. sky

7. shy

8. pry

9. dry

10. my

11. huge

12. giant

13. bulge

Story Words

14. under

    wel come
15. welcome

24

Once upon a time a huge giant sat under a tree. He was so sad ! He was crying and crying and crying.

A little fly came by. "Why do you cry?" said the fly.

"I cannot tell a lie and I cannot tell you why," said the giant.

"Tell me why and I will try to help you," said the fly.

"You are so little," said
the giant. "You cannot
help a huge giant."

"My tears will not dry.
They run like rain from
the sky. Sob, **sob, sob**!
So I will tell you why I
cry. I am very shy!
That is why I feel so
sad. I am **so** shy."

28

"Stop it ! Stop it !" said the little fly. "Just **try** ! You do not have to be shy ! So you do not need to cry !"

"Why ?" said the giant.

"I have a little plan," said the little fly. "Why not try it? You do not have to stay shy. You can be an 'I can try' giant. You will not cry if you try."

"Yes, make me an 'I can try' giant," said the giant.

The little fly said, "OK,
I will help you. See ?
You just pry up the **sh**
from shy."

"Next you must place **tr** in that space. You can read it to me. See it? What will it say?"

"Try," said the giant . . . **"Try**! I can be an **'I can try'** **giant**!"

"Yes, I will try," said
the huge giant. "This is
like a game. It is fun !
I will pry up the **sh** and
set in the **tr**."

"I **did** it!
I am not shy!
I will not cry!
My face is dry!
I **did** it! **I am
an 'I can try'
giant!**"

This made the huge
giant bulge with pride!

35

Thank you, fly!

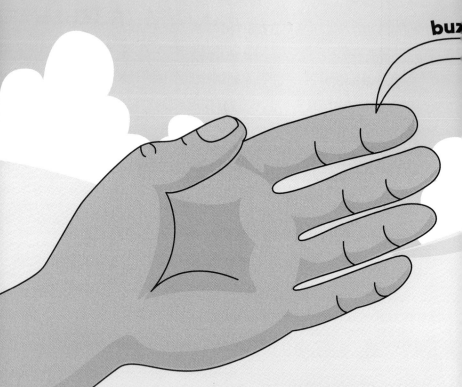

buz

The giant said to the fly, "Wait until my pals see what you did for me!"

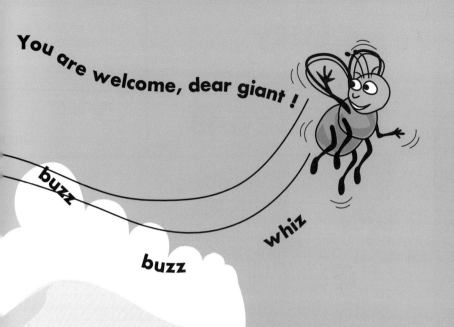

The little fly said with a smile, "See what happens when you try ?"

The End

Lucy and the Jellybeans

Vocabulary

1. Lucy
2. baby
3. Sally
4. pretty
   jelly beans
5. jellybeans
6. happy
7. Billy
8. Gary
9. fussy
10. really

11. funny
12. silly
13. windy
14. buggy

Story Words

    like
15. likes

    sit
16. sits

    up set
17. upset

    thank
18. thanks

Lucy is nine. She likes to baby-sit. She likes to baby-sit Sally. Sally is pretty and she is happy.

"Here, Sally, have some jellybeans," said Lucy. "Red, yellow, pink and green jellybeans."

"I like candy," said Sally, "and I **love** jelly-beans !"

Billy and Gary came up the street.

"Have you seen Freddy ?" said Billy.

"No, he is not here," said Lucy. "He went to fly his kite."

"It is not windy, so he cannot fly a kite," said Gary. "We will wait for him here."

"Have some jellybeans to eat," said Lucy.

"Yes, thank you, Lucy," said Billy and Gary. "We like green jellybeans best."

"Look," said Billy. "I see Freddy. His face is sad."

Freddy had his kite in his hand. He was really upset and fussy.

"It is not funny," he cried. "My kite will not go up !"

"Do not be silly," said Lucy. "It must be windy to fly a kite. Look up at the flag ! See ? No wind, or the flag would wave !"

"Have a jellybean, Freddy. It may make you feel happy," said Lucy.

"Thank you," said Freddy. "I like jellybeans. May I have a red one ?"

"Take two," said Lucy.

"Lucy ! Lucy !
Lucy !" Sally
did yell.

"Dear me ! Sally is
fussy ! I must take her
home for a nap," said Lucy.
"Here is a red jellybean. It
is time to go home. Wave
to Freddy and Billy and
Gary."

Lucy had a big
smile on her face.
Sally had a big
smile on her face.
Jellybeans are nice !

The End

Vocabulary

1. look
2. looking
3. rest
4. rested
5. melt
6. melted
7. camp
8. camped
9. camping
10. jump
11. jumped
12. smile
13. smiled
14. thank
15. thanked
16. pack
17. packed
18. help
19. helped
20. scrubbing
21. mopping
22. rubbing
23. smack
24. smacked
25. race
26. raced
27. back
28. backed
29. licked
30. wave
31. waved
32. honk
33. honked
34. limped
35. leaned
36. fixing
37. jogged
38. jogging
39. paint
40. painted
41. bake
42. baked
43. ice
44. iced
45. played
46. drum
47. drummer
48. drummed
49. drumming
50. batter
51. batted
52. dumped
53. piled
54. hikers
55. hiked
56. mailed
57. locked
58. sailed
59. hopping
60. hopped
61. picked

Story Words

62. saw
63. who
64. ball

47

It was a **hot** day!
Patty and Harry just sat
and rested. Patty licked
a pop. Harry licked a
pop, too! The pops
melted fast!

Daddy came home.
He said, "We have not
camped yet this summer.
Your mommy and I will
take you camping."

49

Patty and Harry jumped
up. They yelled, "That
will be fun ! Thank you,
Daddy."

Daddy smiled and said,
"It is nice to be thanked."

50

Mommy said, "I just baked and iced a cake. We can take it with us."

Daddy smacked his lips. "M-mmm !"

"We can get packed fast," Mommy said. "We will leave at sunrise."

Patty and Harry helped Mommy pack.

Patty and Harry got up at sunrise. They raced to the camper. Mommy got in humming a happy tune. Daddy backed the camper into the street, and off they went !

"Let's look and see what we can see," said Mommy.

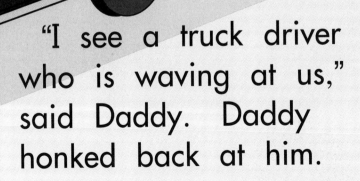

"I see a truck driver who is waving at us," said Daddy. Daddy honked back at him. 53

"I see a man painting
an ad !" yelled Patty.

Next, Mom saw a kid who played his flute and a drummer who was drumming his drum. He drummed a fast beat.

Harry yelled, "I see a baseball game ! A batter has batted the ball and is running to the base."

"I see three kids," yelled Patty, "and one is jumping rope !"

Next, a red truck
dumped sand in a big
pile. The sand piled
up fast.

"See the truck dumping
sand," said Daddy.

"I can see a little tot who is sailing her boat in a stream," said Mommy.

A bunny was hopping by the road.

"I see a bunny," said Daddy. Daddy honked at it. The bunny hopped to a safe place.

"Look !" yelled Harry.
"I see a kid picking up
a rock. When we get to
camp we can look for
rocks, too," he said.

A man limped up the road. He leaned on a stick.

"I see a man with a stick," said Mommy.

A man was fixing a tire.

"I see a man fixing a tire," said Daddy.

60

A flag waved at the top of a hill. A man jogged up the hill.

"I see a flag waving on top of the hill and a man jogging," said Patty.

"Daddy is a jogger too," said Mommy.

"Jogging keeps me in shape," said Daddy.

61

"I see two hikers who have hiked up a steep hill," yelled Harry. "They are puffing and puffing to make it."

"I see a lady who is mailing a letter," said Mommy.

"Look," said Patty. "A kid locked up his bike."

click

"At last we are getting near the camp," said Mom. "There was so much to look at on the way !"

"Yes, we did see a lot," said Harry.

"Looking on the way was fun !" said Patty.

"I see our camp," Daddy said. Patty clapped and Harry yelled, "Yippee !"

The End